IMAGES
of America

MUSCLE SHOALS

The Tennessee River flows through the heart of Muscle Shoals. This photograph, taken in the 1960s, shows an aerial view of Muscle Shoals, including the Wilson Dam and Power Plant. (Photograph courtesy of Tennessee Valley Authority [TVA].)

ON THE COVER: Life in "the Shoals" was around long before it became an incorporated city. After its incorporation in 1923, the town began to grow, as predicted as far back as the late 1700s. In this 1920s shot, proud citizens of the community surround the first official Muscle Shoals Post Office. (Photograph courtesy of TVA.)

IMAGES
of America

MUSCLE SHOALS

Laura Flynn Tapia and Yoshie Lewis

ARCADIA
PUBLISHING

Published by Arcadia Publishing
Charleston, South Carolina

Library of Congress Catalog Card Number: 2007929416

For all general information contact Arcadia Publishing at:
Telephone 843-853-2070
Fax 843-853-0044
E-mail sales@arcadiapublishing.com
For customer service and orders:
Toll-Free 1-888-313-2665

Visit us on the Internet at www.arcadiapublishing.com

In 1918, official construction began on the Wilson Dam. The project brought tens of thousands to the area for employment. The labor was hard, and the living conditions were less than accommodating. Still, they came. These men are working on one of the turbines in its early stage. Note the ranger at the top of the photograph. (Photograph courtesy of TVA.)

CONTENTS

ACKNOWLEDGMENTS

Many thanks to Jesse Bradford, who spent time sharing personal experiences and stories about the history of his hometown. Next, special appreciation goes to Louise Huddleston, archivist at the University of North Alabama (UNA) library, who was so helpful with researching collections and historical documents. Many of these resources would not have been included without William McDonald's contribution of his extensive research to the library.

In addition, thanks to David Hood for so freely sharing the history of which he played such an integral part and for sharing the photographs taken by Tommy Wright for the studio. Thank you Dick Cooper for the images from your extensive collection. A big thanks goes to the Drive-By Truckers, Adam Smith, Luisa Oswalt, Darwin and Jo Ann Bridges, Brad Crisler, Suzanne Bolton, Richard Sheridan, Margy Roark, Lee and Bridgett Flynn, and Landon Flynn. Finally thanks to the Library of Congress, the Tennessee Valley Authority, FAME Studio, and the National Archives for their contributions.

Laura would like to give personal thanks to her parents, husband, and son, whose unfailing support made her work on this book possible. Yoshie is grateful to Richard Carter, who first introduced her to Muscle Shoals and the W. C. Handy Festival.

INTRODUCTION

As early as 1769, and many times since, the words "muscle" (mussel) and "shoals" (meaning low water) were used in reference to the local area. This ideal location, chosen by Native Americans for settlement, offered an abundant supply of mussels, fresh-water streams, forest, and wild game for sustenance. Phrases like "the Muscle Shoals," "at the Muscle Shoals," or "the Shoals" were used by many historians for years to define the area, but it would not be until April 4, 1923, that the words "Muscle Shoals" were used for the name of a city.

Early records indicate that the shoals of the Tennessee River extend upstream a distance of 36 miles. Without this natural phenomenon, it is possible that the Township of Muscle Shoals might never have been established.

There are three legends concerning the origin of the name Muscle Shoals. One is that the interpretation of the Native American language as "it took many muscle to cross shoals." Second is the fact that many mussel shells were found at the shoals. The third is that, while looking at a map of the area, an arm and muscle of a man is quite evident in the shape of the Tennessee River at the shoals.

I am prone to believe the first legend. If the second were correct, then we would have Mussel Shoals as the name of the city. While the shape of a man's arm can be seen in maps prior to the existence of Pickwick Lake, the third reason was made more visible after the construction of Pickwick Dam, which was after the words Muscle Shoals were already used as the city name.

Born a few years after the incorporation of Muscle Shoals as a township, I witnessed first hand the amazing growth of my city. Growing up on my grandfather's farm during the Depression years of the 1930s, I was unaware that I was actually living within the city limits of Muscle Shoals. I have retired to the site of my birthplace and stand in awe of the changes that surround me. I was part of the families comprising the population around Houston Crossroads, the site of Okolona Church and School (the first to be organized within what is now known as Muscle Shoals). Early records indicate the involvement of many of my family members during the formative years of the city. As of this writing, there are many relatives in its employ.

Presently city planners are encouraging the development of the city along Avalon Avenue, which currently houses city hall, the public library, the $5 million high school complex, the police and fire departments, and churches, banks, and other businesses. It is interesting that Avalon was never a designated street in the original plans for the town, much like Muscle Shoals was never intended to become a town.

—Jesse Bradford

One

BEFORE THERE
WAS A TOWN

A diary entry from DeSoto's campaign
through what is now Alabama records
him passing the River of Chicasa (the
Tennessee River at Muscle Shoals),
on December 14, 1540. The river was
flowing out of its bed. (Photograph
courtesy of Library of Congress.)

William McIntosh, a Creek Indian, gained the enmity of Alabama's Upper Creeks by leading Andrew Jackson's troops during the Creek War of 1813–1814. The Upper Creeks were defeated. Some years later, a party of some 200 Creeks killed McIntosh in a raid of retaliation on his plantation. (Photograph courtesy of Library of Congress.)

In addition to the infamy of the wars he campaigned and the 1830 Indian Removal Bill, Andrew Jackson made speculative land purchases in the area dating to 1816. This would not be the last of the many speculative purchases made in the Shoals area over the years. (Photograph courtesy of Library of Congress.)

The Northern Alabama area was inhabited by people dating back well into the BC era. Of the groups that developed, the Creeks (Muskogees) were the largest. The Choctaws and Chikasaws had hunting grounds here for centuries, and the Cherokees claimed land in northeast Alabama. At one time, there were roughly 25 recorded Creek towns and lesser villages. Thus they existed until the Indian Removal Bill, when they were sorrowfully exiled to territories west. The present Echota Cherokee Tribe is descended from landowners who were protected by treaties of 1817 and 1819. (Photograph courtesy of Library of Congress.)

In addition to Andrew Jackson and John Coffee, James Madison was one of the stockholders in the Cypress Land Company. They purchased 5,515 acres from the government and speculated that the area was sure to become one of the largest commercial towns. (Photograph courtesy of Library of Congress.)

The Forks of Cypress belonged to James Jackson. It was constructed between 1816 and 1820 and was home to three of the four horses to whom the modern American Thoroughbred is credited: Galopade, Glencoe, and the legendary Leviathan. The home burned in 1966. Notice the eerie, jockey-like shadow above the door. (Photographs courtesy of Library of Congress.)

Irish-born James Jackson moved his home from Nashville to the area in 1819, obtaining his prime land in the sales after the Creek Wars. Living at the Forks of Cypress, his new home near Florence, Jackson energetically planted cotton and flax, raised livestock, and invested in textile mills—some of his own design—on the tributaries of the Tennessee River. He invested in a number of other business enterprises, served in the Alabama House of Representatives and in the senate as president, and raised 11 children with his wife, Sarah. He also imported horses. (Photograph courtesy of Library of Congress.)

Pictured is a present stretch of the original Jackson Military Road. It was constructed between 1817 and 1822 and shortened the route from Nashville to New Orleans by 200 miles. It was later renamed Jackson Highway, the namesake for the famous studio and album by Cher. (Photograph courtesy of author.)

On March 3, 1817, the Alabama Territory was created. It was formed from the eastern portion of Mississippi shortly before Mississippi became a state. The town of St. Stephens became the official seat. Alabama's population increased sufficiently, and so Pres. James Monroe signed the enabling act for statehood on March 2, 1819. Alabama became the 22nd state on December 14, 1819. (Photograph courtesy of Library of Congress.)

The area's first steamboat, the *Alabama*, was constructed in St. Stephens. After its first trip to Mobile, it did not even have enough steam to make it back. It began a new era in transportation, and the progress in harnessing and navigating river power became unstoppable. (Photograph courtesy of UNA Library Collection.)

Originally this cabin was on a piece of property that was jointly owned by John Hickman and Benjamin Sherrod. Little is known of Hickman save that he took ownership in 1818 and worked the some 2,000 acres until he sold his portion to Sherrod. (Photograph courtesy of Library of Congress.)

Benjamin Sherrod served in the War of 1812 as a contractor with the Commissary Department. He established Pond Spring after acquiring the property from John Hickman. He was known for his great attention to soil preservation in cotton farming and for his interest in the Tuscumbia, Courtland, and Decatur Railway. (Photograph courtesy of Library of Congress.)

Because of the unnavigable nature of the Tennessee River, planters needed a railroad to serve as an "iron river." In 1832, the Tuscumbia, Courtland, and Decatur Railway was established. At a completed cost of $429,000, it spanned 43 miles. One of its originators, David Hubbard, traveled all the way to Pennsylvania to study one of the early railroad experiments. The railroad's first president was Benjamin Sherrod. (Photograph courtesy of Library of Congress.)

Belle Mont, also known as the Isaac Winston House and Henry B. Thornton Plantation, saw its heyday c. 1825–1849. It was built in what is now Colbert County. The fields shown are raped from years of cotton harvesting. Plantations of this magnitude were supported by slave labor. Huge buyers, such as Calvert Roberts of New Orleans, kept office in the district. (Photograph courtesy of Library of Congress.)

Established by the Methodist Church, La Grange College was Alabama's first chartered college. There was a division, and in 1855, it became Florence Wesleyan University and moved locations. That portion eventually became what is now the University of Northern Alabama. Women were admitted in 1874, and it became the first coeducational teacher training school. (Photograph courtesy of UNA.)

At the other side of the college's division, located on the original property, three slaves were hired in 1857 to form the drum and bugle corps at what became La Grange Military Academy officially in 1860. It closed its doors in 1862 and was burned in 1863 by "Cornyn's Angels," who were part of the Union army. (Photograph courtesy of UNA.)

Excavation on the Muscle Shoals Canal began in 1881. Spoils were shoveled into railcars running on temporary tracks laid at the bottom of the canal section. The workforce was almost entirely black. (Photograph courtesy of UNA Library Collection.)

This November 8, 1895, photograph shows the progress on the pit and south wall of the lift lock. (Photograph courtesy of UNA Library Collection.)

In 1871, the government had appropriated funds for the construction of the canal. The actual cost at start-up was $100,000. In May 1872, Maj. Walter McFarland of the Army Corps of Engineers made the first survey. The old canal of the 1830s was widened by 70 feet. (Photographs courtesy of UNA Library Collection.)

Constant dredging was required by boats like the dredge *Indiana* in order to keep the canal clear enough for passage of other vessels. There is an abundant amount of silt in the Tennessee River, and it was a formidably impossible task to prevent it from infiltrating the canal. (Photographs courtesy of UNA Library Collection.)

The canal opened on the November 10, 1890, after 15 years of construction. The total cost was a staggering $3 million. The first successful voyage occurred when a steamboat traveled from St. Louis to Chattanooga on November 10, 1890. (Photograph courtesy of TVA.)

This is a view of Lock 4 taken in July 1877. After a revision in 1877 by Maj. W. R. King that modified the original survey and reduced the number of locks from 17 to 9, Lt. Col. George Washington Goethals, former engineer for Sherman's army, took the project in hand. He later left to become the chief engineer for the Panama Canal. Also pictured is the south wall of the lift lock, taken May 18, 1900. (Photographs courtesy of UNA Library Collection.)

This December 7, 1898, photograph shows the south wall of the lift lock. The May 13, 1900, photograph below shows the completed masonry on the lift lock. The completed canal fell 85 feet in 14.5 miles. It was closed in 1918 and later was covered by water from the Wilson and Wheeler Dams. (Photographs courtesy of UNA Library Collection.)

Pictured are another dredge boat and tug. One tug, the *City of Chattanooga*, sank twice while pushing four coal barges. (Photograph courtesy of UNA Library Collection.)

To aid in construction, a 14-mile railroad track was built on the south levy. It was later utilized to tow boats through the canal. (Photograph courtesy of UNA Library Collection.)

The Florence Bridge was built in 1840. After being damaged by a storm, it was reopened in 1853. Again it was damaged by a tornado in 1854 and not opened again for use until 1860. It was burned in 1862 to deter the Union troops. By the end of the war, the Shoals had changed hands 40 times. (Above, photograph courtesy of TVA; below, photograph courtesy of UNA Library Collection.)

Armistead Barton built Cunningham Plantation c. 1848 at the cost of $25,000 and additional slave labor. By the 1830s, Alabama was becoming the largest producer of cotton, the largest product turned out by plantations such as these. This 1936 photograph shows the smokehouse. The main house is captured in a 1935 shot. (Photographs courtesy of Library of Congress.)

The slave quarters from Cunningham Plantation are depicted in this image, taken in 1935. Parker Poole, a former slave from the area, was photographed in 1937. Historical records do not indicate when the first slaves were brought into the Muscle Shoals area. But long before Alabama became a state in the Union, forces were at work to establish slavery in northwest Alabama. The French, Spanish, and British, who claimed the Shoals area at various times, all accepted the practice of slavery in their colonial territories. (Photographs courtesy of Library of Congress.)

Slaves picked cotton under the watchful eye of the overseer, c. 1860. While cotton exports totaled only $5 million in 1800 (7 percent of total U.S. exports), they rose to $30 million in 1830 (41 percent of U.S. exports) and reached $191 million in 1860 (57 percent of total U.S. exports). Southerners, whether or not they owned slaves, equated wealth, economic security, and power with slaveholding. The slave quarters at Forks of Cypress, the plantation of James Jackson, were photographed in 1935. Parson Dick, the groom and handler of the estate's thoroughbreds, possibly inhabited these quarters. (Photographs courtesy of Library of Congress.)

This yard of the Oaks, another plantation in the region before there was a Muscle Shoals, was used for such chores as making candles, soap, and syrup. Such tasks required a large, outdoor area for large fires and cook pots. This work was also done by slave labor. (Photograph courtesy of Library of Congress.)

Cotton barges such as this were a typical sight in pre–Civil War Alabama. They would have been towed down the river to other ports for trade. (Photographs courtesy of UNA Library Collection.)

During the War Between the States, Pond Spring was a favorite camping ground for both armies. Gen. Joseph Wheeler completed this house after the war. In June 1864, Confederate colonel Josiah Patterson of Morgan County used Pond Spring as his headquarters. This cook's house might have been used by the Union as a parole headquarters for Confederates. (Photographs courtesy of Library of Congress.)

Gen. Joseph "Fighting Joe" Wheeler was one of the youngest Confederate generals. Some records indicate that 16 horses were shot out from under him. He married Daniella Sherrod Jones in 1866 and took over Pond Spring. He was later a commander in the Spanish-American War and was elected to Congress in 1880. He is one of the few Confederates buried in Arlington Cemetery. (Photograph courtesy of Library of Congress.)

The remains of the formerly glamorous Pond Spring are pictured in the 1930s. Annie Early Wheeler, born in 1868, spent her days here as the second of General Wheeler's children. In 1898, she followed her brother and father to Cuba during the Spanish-American War. There she earned the title of "Angel of Santiago" after being placed in charge of a hospital by Clara Barton, the first president of the Red Cross. (Photographs courtesy of Library of Congress.)

Colbert County was established as a result of the politics of the aftermath of the War Between the States. It was formalized in 1867 and abolished eight months later. It was reestablished in 1870, and construction began on the courthouse in 1881. Colbert County was named after Chief George Colbert. Both George and his brother Levi were Chickasaw chiefs. George set up operation of Colbert's Ferry in 1798 at the mouth of Bear Creek on what was the otherwise uncrossable Tennessee River. (Photograph courtesy of Colbert County.)

On March 11, 1881, $5,002 was robbed from the paymaster as he left the bank to pay workers on the Muscle Shoals Canal near Lock 6, pictured below. The perpetrator of the crime was none other than the infamous outlaw Jesse James. (Right, photograph courtesy of Library of Congress; below, photograph courtesy of UNA Library Collection.)

The steamboat *Joe Wheeler*, pictured above, was built in Chicago and carried passengers and freight until 1918. At that time, the cabin was cut down, and it became a tow boat. In 1919, it was fully dismantled. Steamboats were the primary means of transportation for many years while cotton was king and before the canal was built. (Photographs courtesy of UNA Library Collection.)

Even after the Civil War, steamboats were still a popular mode of travel. Folks are gathered at the Riverton Lock in both photographs. The structure is an operations building for the lock. (Photographs courtesy of UNA Library Collection.)

One of the most important ingredients of industrialization was the railroad. Before the war, the Tennessee Valley had three major lines, the Memphis and Charleston being the largest and most important. After the war, the company suffered continuous financial problems and was forced into foreclosure in February 1898. On July 1, 1898, it was absorbed and operated as the Southern Railroad. (Photograph courtesy of UNA Library Collection.)

On February 24, 1879, the Nashville and Florence Railroad was incorporated in Tennessee. Eight years later, on January 19, 1887, the Tennessee and Alabama Railroad was formed to connect Sheffield and Florence via the railroad bridge. No work was ever done, and the company was consolidated with the Nashville and Florence Company in May 1887 to form the Nashville, Florence, and Sheffield Railroad. (Photograph courtesy of UNA Library Collection.)

The fall of 1922 saw the end of the railroad strike that affected workers like these. The strike began when the Railroad Labor Board announced that wages would be cut by 7¢ an hour beginning on July 1. Many shop men made concessions and negotiated independently, causing hard relations between the shop workers and the railroads for quite some time. (Photograph courtesy of UNA Library Collection.)

Trolleys were a popular mode of travel prior to and during World War I in the Shoals area. Each car carried 60 to 70 people and was often packed. The trolley traveled 60 feet above the river on the bridge and varied in cost from 5¢ to 15¢, depending on the route traveled. (Photographs courtesy of UNA Library Collection.)

In the winter of 1917–1918 there was a cold snap causing the Tennessee River to freeze. On January 12, 1918, the temperature dropped to eight degrees below zero, causing all construction to come to a halt on the new nitrate plant project. (Photograph courtesy of UNA Library Collection.)

Pictured is the Tennessee River at high tide January 27, 1919, just one year after the river had ice floating on it. This is the cofferdam that was used to hold back water from a portion of the construction on the Wilson Dam. The water was so high that it overflowed the temporary structure. There were a total of six cofferdams built over two miles. (Photograph courtesy of TVA Retirees.)

The Sheffield Hotel, pictured around 1920, was one of the locations where Henry Ford and Thomas Edison stayed when prospecting the area. Known as the "center of the Shoals," Sheffield made a convenient location to access Florence, Tuscumbia, and most importantly, Muscle Shoals. The two arrived in Florence by Ford's private train, *Fairlane*. They stayed for three days. (Photograph courtesy of UNA Library Collection.)

Two

TVA AND THE WILSON DAM

A 1918 photograph includes Word Glasgow (second row at left), who later became mayor of Tishomingo, Mississippi. This photograph shows workers perched on rail tracks. The same year, the deadly influenza epidemic hit the nation, killing nearly 50,000 people. Some 8,000 were afflicted in the Shoals area, and numerous laborers, primarily foreigners, were buried on the construction site. Some of these workers are reported as being from as far away as Cuba, but the language barrier made informing families of their relatives' deaths difficult, and so it rarely occurred. (Photograph courtesy of Jack Epperson.)

"If the drop of the river had not been so dramatic at this exact spot, Muscle Shoals might not exist at all," says local historian Jesse Bradford. This image shows a surveyor evaluating a possible dam site in 1917. This decision marks the beginning of a new era for the Muscle Shoals area. (Photograph courtesy of TVA Retirees.)

Rockwood Quarry, pictured in August 1918, was a primary source of materials for the dam construction. It was conveniently in the vicinity of the dam site, making it a logical choice. (Photograph courtesy of UNA Library Collection.)

Ronald D. Young and Earl H. Brown extensively researched the construction of the nitrate plants and determined it would require an average of 111 railcars of construction equipment and materials each day to complete the structures. This meant that a total of 31,000 carloads would be required. (Photographs courtesy of TVA Retirees.)

In 1898, Rep. Joe Wheeler introduced a bill to Congress to construct a power plant. It was the first of many bills of its sort. On March 3, 1899, Pres. William McKinley signed a bill allowing Muscle Shoals Power Company to construct a dam. It was later vetoed by Teddy Roosevelt. (Photograph courtesy of TVA Retirees.)

In 1914, Congress approved $20 million for the construction of two plants to test the processing of nitrates. One plant used the German Haber process, which had recently been stolen by the British and offered to America for experimentation. The plants were to produce some 22,000 tons, and ground was broken in October 1917. (Photograph courtesy of TVA Retirees.)

The Tennessee River, dammed at Muscle Shoals, was projected to have the potential to produce 680,000 kilowatts of electricity. That is more than two times the capacity of Niagara Falls. The ground-breaking was on August 18, 1918, but the construction of the dam would not be completed until after the war. Only 35 percent of the project was completed when construction was halted for the duration of the war, with just two of the eight generators running. (Photographs courtesy of TVA Retirees.)

At the peak of its construction, the Wilson Dam and nitrate plant projects employed more than 18,000 workers and utilized 1,700 temporary buildings, 185 residential units, and 685 miles of electrical cable. (Photographs courtesy of TVA Retirees.)

Word Muldrow Glasgow (sixth from the left in the second row) was a math teacher before he came to work on Wilson Dam. After his stint as a day laborer, he moved to Tishomingo, Mississippi, and became mayor. This photograph was taken in 1918. (Photograph courtesy of Jack Epperson.)

Pictured on March 11, 1919, are the wash and locker room (above) and the officers' quarters near nitrate plant No. 2. So huge was the number of employees that it became necessary to build what was virtually a small town to facilitate the workers' daily needs. (Photographs courtesy of UNA Library Collection.)

The ordnance barracks area was home to thousands of men during construction. The second photograph shows the mess halls to the left and the motion picture theater at the end of the street. These facilities were for Nitrate Plant No. 2 and were captured in these shots on March 11, 1919. (Photographs courtesy of UNA Library Collection.)

One of the white mess halls was photographed on March 19, 1918. The kitchen pictured was for white mess hall No. 5. The shot below is from May 23, 1918. There were 23 military-style mess halls that fed some 20,000 workers. That was more than 24,000 meals a day on average. One day's meals might have included 750 gallons of soup, 18 bushels of potatoes, 2 tons of meat, 13,000 loaves of bread, 1,000 pies, 1,200 cakes, 700 cinnamon rolls, and 150 gallons of pudding. In one particular 48-hour period, 30,000 pounds of meat was cooked. (Photographs courtesy of UNA Library Collection.)

The Muscle Shoals Nitrate Plant police department is pictured. Officer Harry S. White lost his life in the line of duty on December 7, 1923, when he was shot and killed by poachers at Nitrate Plant No. 1. Officer White ordered a pair of poachers to break their shotguns and walk ahead of his horse, but when his attention was distracted by the poachers' dogs, one of the men swung around and shot and killed the officer. The two men then robbed Officer White's body of his wallet and service revolver before hiding the body and fleeing. Both men were arrested a short time later. One of the suspects was executed by hanging on October 9, 1925. (Photograph courtesy of UNA Library Collection.)

Henry Ford and Thomas Edison visited the Shoals in a speculative move after Pres. Warren Harding's administration decided to sell the dam in 1921. Henry Ford offered to lease the dam and buy the nitrate plants. In another offer, he told Congress that he would buy the dam for $5 million. He was turned down. The initial cost alone for the dam was $46.5 million. He boasted that he would employ 1 million people and build a city 75 miles long. People from all over bought lots, sight unseen. (Photographs courtesy of Library of Congress.)

In addition to the hydroelectric generating system, steam plants were also built. This one, adjacent to Nitrate Plant No. 2, could generate about 80,000 additional horsepower. Coal was plentiful, allowing these plants to run economically at low water. (Photograph courtesy of TVA Retirees.)

So massive was the requirement for board feet for form work on the dam that a lumberyard was set up specifically to fill that need. (Photograph courtesy of UNA Library Collection.)

This photograph was taken in 1918 of the filter plant at Nitrate Plant No. 2. On November 16, 1917, the government announced Muscle Shoals would receive the second plant to experiment with the American Cynamid process. This announcement virtually ensured the construction of a massive hydroelectric dam. Nitrate Plant No. 2 would require 2,300 acres and was estimated to produce 110,000 tons of nitrates annually. (Photograph courtesy UNA Library Collection.)

The permanent power plant at Wilson Dam is pictured in its early days. The plant was used to process and disperse the power harnessed by the dam from the Tennessee River. (Photograph courtesy of TVA Retirees.)

This photograph from June 3, 1928, shows men at the concreting process for the bridge pier recesses. This was at the spillway for the dam. (Photograph courtesy of TVA Retirees.)

The Wilson Dam is shown on February 26, 1926, in full operation. This view of the dam is from Jackson Island. (Photograph courtesy of TVA Retirees.)

The steamer *McPherson* and a dredge boat are shown in Upper Chamber Lock No. 2's upper level on March 5, 1926. The dam construction continued to improve the navigation of the shoals for watercraft. (Photograph courtesy of UNA Library Collection.)

Increased automobile traffic required bridges. Wilson Dam opened in 1925, giving drivers an alternative to the old railroad bridge. During the Great Depression, the state floated a bond issue to build a new, four-lane bridge. (Photographs courtesy of TVA Retirees.)

Pres. Franklin D. Roosevelt came to Muscle Shoals on January 21, 1933, to evaluate the federal government's position on the proposed TVA site. Consequently he signed the act creating TVA on May 18 of that same year. This controversial moment in the history of Muscle Shoals is commemorated in this photograph. (Photograph courtesy of TVA Retirees.)

"Our people and our families remember what he [Roosevelt] did for us here in the Muscle Shoals region. I think it is fitting that we pay tribute to him for lifting us out of despair," says Mildred Hensley. Hensley, among others, is raising funds to create a memorial for FDR. Many strongly believe he saved the area during the Great Depression by creating employment with the introduction of the Tennessee Valley Authority. (Photograph courtesy of TVA Retirees.)

These two photographs show men working on the turbines for the dam. The above image was taken in 1918 and the below in the 1960s. By the 1930s, most of the homes in the Muscle Shoals vicinity were still without electricity despite the earlier construction of the dam. The turbines were placed the in tunnels of the dam to facilitate the production of power. This power made it possible to have lights and modern appliances. By the end of World War II, TVA was the nation's largest power supplier, and the majority of the area had electricity. (Photographs courtesy of TVA Retirees.)

Alonzo Bankston was an operator in the TVA plant that produced carbide for use in other plants manufacturing synthetic rubber. (Photograph courtesy of Library of Congress.)

This man is working at one of the electric phosphate smelting furnaces. The phosphorus, used in the manufacture of incendiary bombs and shells and of material for "smoke," was produced in the electric furnaces. When surplus phosphorus was available, it was converted into highly concentrated phosphate fertilizer, much of which was shipped abroad under provisions of the Lend-Lease Bill. (Photograph courtesy of Library of Congress.)

Touted as FDR's boldest and most liberal social planning experiment, the Wilson Dam project was still unsuccessful at accomplishing better racial integration and equal rights, despite the efforts of national and valley civil rights organizations. In spite of high wages of 30¢ per hour, worker shortages occurred. It is reported that 80,000 people were hired to keep 20,000 actually working. The high turnover rate was attributed to poor living conditions, housing shortages, price gouging, and racial discrimination against the some 7,000 black workers. (Photograph courtesy of TVA Retirees.)

From left to right, Paul L. Imes, Samuel C. Watkins, and George W. Richardson were employed as lab technicians in 1942. They were among those who rose to better opportunity, despite the difficult circumstances posed by the social mores of the period. (Photograph courtesy of Library of Congress.)

In 1945, Jean-Paul Sartre (seated at far right) came to Muscle Shoals, not as the existentialist he is known for being but as a journalist for French magazines. Sartre and seven other representatives were guests of the U.S. War Department. They arrived in a B-29 bomber in Knoxville. After visiting other sites, they flew to Muscle Shoals. (Photograph courtesy of Library of Congress.)

From July 1956 to November 1957, a single lift lock was built to aid in additional boating traffic on the river. It was 110 feet by 600 feet. By the 1960s, electric rates in the Shoals were among the nation's lowest thanks to the Wilson Dam. The below photograph shows the completed lock in use in 1968. Note the size of the boat in relation to the size of the lock. (Above, photograph courtesy of TVA Retirees; below, photograph courtesy of Library of Congress.)

Three

EVERYDAY LIVING

In the late 1800s, the Muscle Shoals community was growing around what was known as Houston Crossroads, now the intersection of Sixth Street and Wilson Dam Road. Jerry Schlullentoffer, a German Catholic living in Tuscumbia, deeded one acre and appointed W. M. Counts and Mr. McKinney as trustees of the school. Farmers cut timber from their property and built a very small building, Okolona School. The following year, 1896, the building was used by various church denominations. This continued until 1898, when Okolona Baptist Church was established. The members got the name from a group of travelers passing through from Okolona, Mississippi. (Photograph courtesy of Jesse Bradford.)

Open cotton fields dotted with cabins and barns, like these from 1936, filled the landscape during the early development of the Muscle Shoals area. Growth progressed slowly during the first 20 years of incorporation, beginning in 1923. There were only 1,113 people in Muscle Shoals proper by 1940. Industrial growth sparked the steady expansion of the town in the 1950s with Reynolds Metals Company, Union Carbide Metals, Diamond Shamrock Company, and Ford Motor Company among others. (Photographs courtesy of Library of Congress.)

Religion was a primary part of life in the Deep South, with both whites and slaves attending regular church services. The Muscle Shoals Baptist Association, in its eighth-annual session in 1827, stated, "The brethren, who own servants do release them from their labor on that day (of worship) and carry them and their wives and their little ones to engage in worship of the Most High." Initially they worshipped in shared meetinghouses, although there was separate seating for blacks, usually in the back of the sanctuary. In 1858, the Muscle Shoals Baptist Association reported a membership of 3,306 whites and 753 blacks. (Photograph courtesy of UNA Library Collection.)

In the 1920s, there were a few former-slave ministers and one black-controlled church, but continual white restraints were placed on their ability to minister and meet. A group of aldermen in the Shoals area ordered the constable "to put a stop to and prohibit the negroes from holding preaching and other gatherings" within city limits. December 1848 brought about another prohibition from the aldermen stating that there would be "no negro preaching and prayer meetings," and "no negro may preach except Dick Kirkman," but this was permitted only in the daytime. (Photograph courtesy of UNA Library Collection.)

Union Church was located in the "Colored Village." Photographed is the pastor of the congregation. Like the town outside the confines of the nitrate villages, the church served as one of the primary social outlets for the community. Worshipping with whites was permitted at this time, but by establishing racially segregated churches, blacks were offered greater individual freedom and expression, which was impossible in local, white churches that continued to retain racist attitudes. (Photograph courtesy of UNA Library Collection.)

This photograph shows a schoolhouse and its students in the Colored Village. One local historian recalls workers being brought in from as far as Cuba to work on the nitrate plant. The two girls in the fourth row may have been children of these laborers. During the flu epidemic, many died, and the language barrier made it difficult if not impossible to notify families of the loss of their loved ones. (Photograph courtesy of TVA.)

Although the attempt at racial integration was politically significant within this community of workers, the initial division by color was apparent. Separate village areas and designated white entrances at the movie theater and other buildings marked this early period for employees and their families. (Photograph courtesy of UNA Library Collection.)

After work comes play or, sometimes, discontent. Both are only natural given the close quarters most employees shared. Not only did they work together, they also ate, slept, and lived within the confines of these prefabricated villages created by TVA. (Above, photograph courtesy of TVA; below, photograph courtesy of UNA Library Collection.)

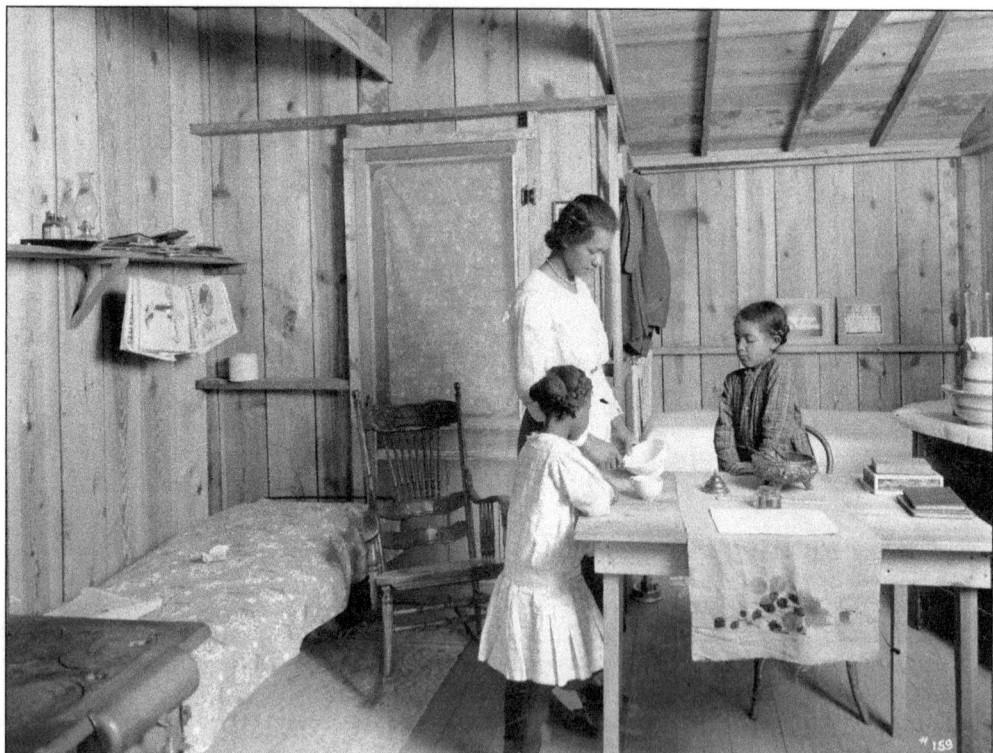

"The striking thing is the lightness, the fragility of these buildings. The village has no weight . . . it has not managed to leave a human imprint on the reddish earth and the dark forest," said French existentialist Jean-Paul Sartre when he visited TVA in Oak Ridge and viewed the temporary housing, much like the housing that he also viewed here. (Photographs courtesy of UNA Library Collection.)

During World War I, construction began on Village One to house nitrate plant employees and their families. The first shot is of the construction of the houses on Alabama Street on May 6, 1918. The streets were laid out in an unusual Liberty Bell design and consisted of 85 bungalows, officer's barracks, and a school. Alabama Street actually marks the final location of the legendary Muscle Shoals Sound Studio. The second shot is of the intersection of Alabama and Florence Streets. Alabama Street still exists today in Sheffield, winding through town to the Tennessee River's edge. (Photographs courtesy of UNA Library Collection.)

These images show Alabama Street in 1919, just over a year later, and development was taking place. The above image is the intersection of Greenbriar and Alabama Streets in Industrial Village. The below image shows Alabama Street at Filbert Street. (Photographs courtesy of UNA Library Collection.)

This tree-lined street reveals a quiet Muscle Shoals neighborhood in 1949. At this time, out-of-town real estate investors began to withdraw and sell their properties, enabling local ownership. Many of the plots that were originally purchased during the excitement of Henry Ford's announcement to build a major city in Muscle Shoals had been abandoned and the land overgrown. Locals were able to purchase these sites by just paying the back taxes. This shift stimulated growth and development in the city. (Photograph courtesy of TVA.)

A. L. Howell and C. T. Graves (of New York) were the first city developers. They constructed Howell and Graves School in 1927. The school was designed in the neoclassical style by architect Harry J. Frahn. Noted for its castle-like appearance, the school served a variety of purposes. It was not only an educational facility but also played host to a multitude of special events, like political rallies and community meetings. Local historian Jesse Bradford recalls farmers being taught how to make cotton bedding during after-hour instructional sessions. These 1920s photographs represent the full school and one of the classes. (Photographs courtesy of Luisa Oswalt.)

The Crossroads school, mentioned earlier in this chapter, was used until 1927, when Howell and Graves opened, accommodating students from grades one to nine. Each year, one grade was added. Pictured above is the fourth-grade class of 1948–1949 (fifth from the left is Lee Roy Oswalt). In the photograph below, of one of the younger classes is shown. Lacking a large enough area to hold graduation services, the first graduating class of Muscle Shoals held their commencement ceremony at Woodward Avenue Baptist Church. The City of Muscle Shoals and the Colbert County Historical Landmarks Foundation erected the Howell and Graves historical marker on December 4, 2006, along with a dedication ceremony to mark the significant role the school continues to play in the advancement of Muscle Shoals. (Photographs courtesy of Luisa Oswalt.)

Seeking to improve accommodations for workers and their families, the TVA created a progressive school in the barracks building for employee's children, which was used from 1934 to 1941. Children were encouraged to engage in many different activities to pass the time, not just academics. Eventually the school was donated to the City of Sheffield in 1949. (Photograph courtesy of TVA.)

Multiple villages were constructed to house employees. This particular facility, photographed in 1937, was located in what was called "Village One." The first village in this ambitious endeavor was laid out in the shape of the Liberty Bell. The site of Village One, where the school was located in Colbert County, was recognized as a historical landmark by the Alabama Historical Association in 2005. (Photograph courtesy of TVA.)

At the extreme left is the mess hall that sat beside the police barracks. The nitrate plants had their own police force stationed at Nitrate Plant No. 2. The schoolchildren at the forefront were in the class of 1918–1919. (Photographs courtesy of UNA Library Collection.)

Julia Thorne Sharpton was the first post mistress of the Muscle Shoals Post Office and held this position for 31.5 years. She married Arthur W. Sharpton, who became the second mayor, the first being George McBride. After the untimely death of Mayor Sharpton, Mrs. Sharpton married Henry Green, who also became mayor. She is the only woman to this date to have been married to two mayors in the city of Muscle Shoals. (Photograph courtesy of TVA.)

Ruth Clement Bond was a civil activist and famed quilt maker responsible for the collection known as the "T.V.A. Quilts." Married to J. Max Bond, she moved with him to North Alabama when he was hired to supervise the African American men working on the construction of the dams for the Tennessee Valley Authority. Mrs. Bond created extraordinary designs and, in turn, organized the wives of the segregated workers to sew them. Six quilts were completed in 1934. They named the first in their collection "Black Power." Many believe this is the origin of the "Black Power" slogan. The quilt pictured a black hand holding a lightning bolt, symbolizing the electrical power being created by TVA. Three full-sized quilts from the series are still in existence, as are multiple smaller samples created for the project. "The Lazy Man," another quilt from this collection, has been recognized as one of the top 100 quilts of the 20th century by judges elected from the Alliance for American Quilts, the American Quilt Study Group, the International Quilt Association, and the National Quilt Association. (Photograph courtesy of TVA.)

Queen Mother Audley E. Moore, known as a warrior woman and pivotal figure in the struggle for freedom for African descendents, worked as a volunteer nurse during the great flu epidemic in 1918 in Muscle Shoals, Alabama. The virus affected 46 states killing 500,000 nationally with nearly 8,000 sick in the Shoals area. From her compassionate service in Muscle Shoals, she carried her visionary efforts of equality all the way to the United Nations, presenting petitions against genocide and later in support of land reparations. Befriending such influential figures as Nelson Mandela and Marcus Garvey, her dedication to human and civil rights prompted her role as founder and president of the Universal Association of Ethiopian Women. Since her death in May 1997, she has been remembered as a formidable warrior in the fight for black liberation. (Photograph courtesy of Library of Congress.)

Hugo Black formally announced his intent to run for a seat in the U.S. Senate in the spring of 1926. Intense campaigning took Black to every county in Alabama. In May 1925, near the Muscle Shoals dam, it is said that more than a thousand people stood inside the hangar listening for over two hours. Black stated that the idle dam, which sat only five miles away, should be used to make fertilizer for farmers and electricity for the town. Black's support of the New Deal gained him a favorable reputation with President Roosevelt, who appointed him to the Supreme Court in 1937 despite his prior association with the Ku Klux Klan. (Photograph courtesy of Library of Congress.)

The size of the catfish in the Tennessee River, especially near the dam, is legendary. This c. 1925 image is evidence of how large some have become, fueling the urban legends that still pervade the Shoals area about catfish in the river that are the size of men. Competitive fishing continues to draw anglers from across the nation to this small town in North Alabama to participate in major annual tournaments. (Photograph courtesy of TVA.)

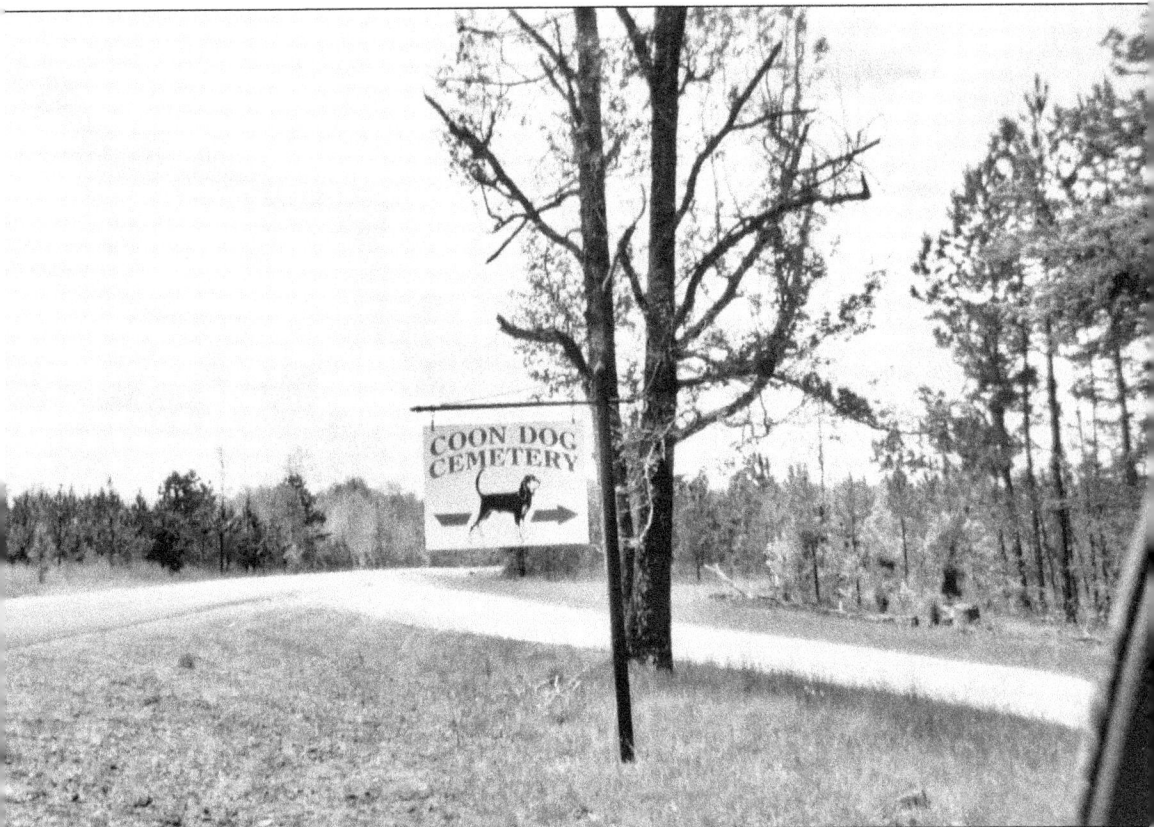

In 1937, Key Underwood buried his faithful coon dog of 15 years. Troop, who was half redbone coonhound and half birdsong, was known through out the region as the best. He was "cold nosed," meaning he could follow cold coon tracks until they grew fresh, and he never left the trail until he had treed the coon. Since that time, nearly 200 coon dogs have been buried in Coon Dog Cemetery, making it one of the area's most unusual attractions. (Photograph courtesy of author.)

The Muscle Shoals airport serviced this area for decades. In the 1940s, one of the Eastern Airline's great silver fleet paid a visit. In addition to passenger travel, they were one of the main relays for mail. (Photograph courtesy of Library of Congress.)

Four

THE MUSIC SCENE

Rick Hall's original recording studio was above the old City Drug store in downtown Florence on the corner of Tennessee and Seminary Streets. In 1961, Hall's partnership with Tom Stafford and Billy Sherrill dissolved, and he set up shop in an old tobacco warehouse across the river in Muscle Shoals. Hall earned enough royalties to build a studio on Avalon Avenue, producing his first hit, Arthur Alexander's "You Better Move On" in the run-down warehouse. (Photograph courtesy of FAME Studios.)

Rick Hall's FAME Studios helped to earn Muscle Shoals the title of the "Hit Recording Capital of the World," as stated on a sign just past the airport. Instinct and hard work earned Hall industry accolades and Billboard's "Producer of the Year" in 1971, among numerous other honors. Accommodating three publishing companies, two recording studios, and a production company, the original studio location continues to thrive. Hall, along with his son Rodney, is still producing hits with some of music's top performers. (Photograph courtesy of David Hood.)

The Fairlanes, the original house band for FAME Studios, was comprised of five members. Pictured from left to right are Rick Hall, Charlie Senn, Randy Allen (drums), Billy Sherrill, and Terri Thompson. (Photograph courtesy of FAME Studios.)

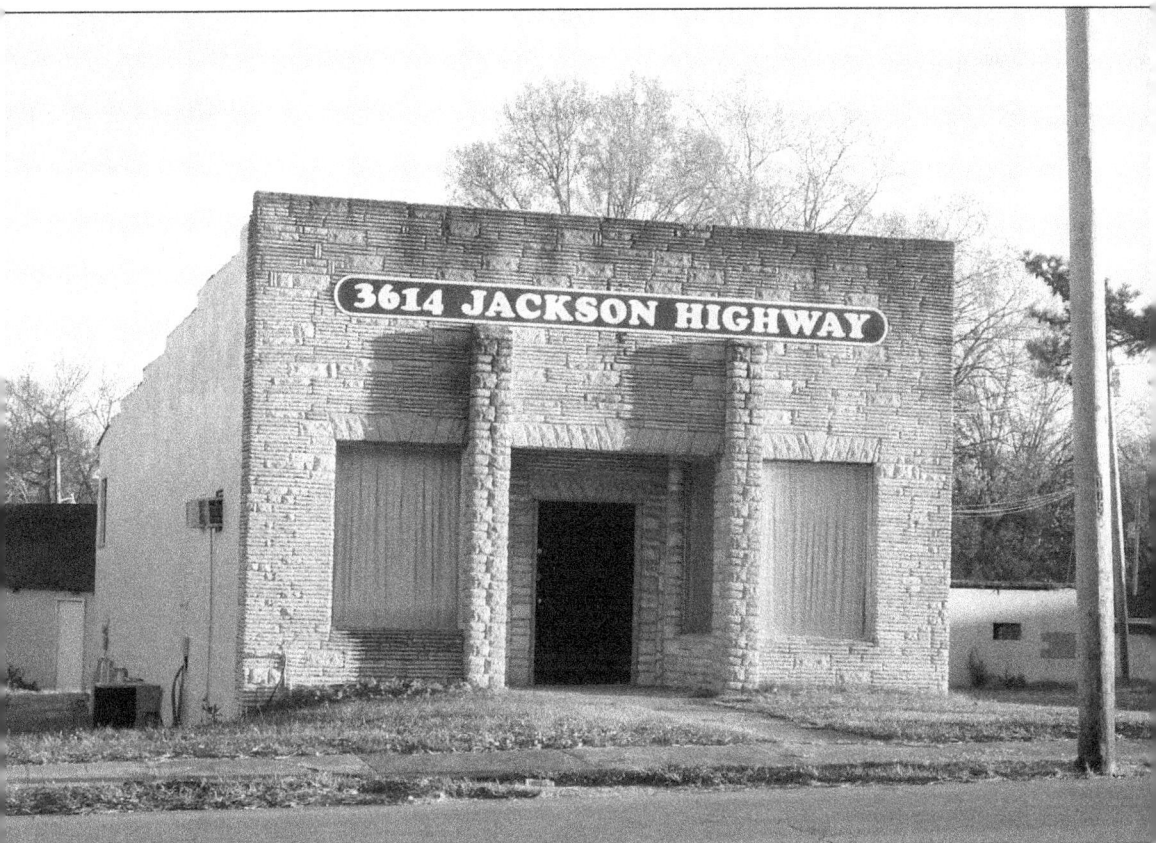

In 1969, the Rhythm Section began their own recording studio, which they named the Muscle Shoals Sound Studio, located at 3614 Jackson Highway. It was home to many artists, including the Swampers, who were forever immortalized in Lynyrd Skynyrd's classic "Sweet Home Alabama" ("Muscle Shoals has got the Swampers"). The Muscle Shoals Rhythm Section has more than this reference to secure their spot among legendary musicians. (Photograph courtesy of Dick Cooper.)

The original Swampers, also known as the Muscle Shoals Rhythm Section, are pictured at FAME. From left to right are Junior Lowe, Roger Hawkins, Barry Beckett, Jimmy Johnson, and David Hood. Bob Seger came to town to record five albums with the Rhythm Section. "Muscle Shoals did the ballads like 'Down on Main Street' better than my band," Seger says. "The wonderful thing about them is the second you started playing the song, it sounded like a record." (Photograph Courtesy of David Hood.)

Legendary producer Rick Hall handpicked the world-class Muscle Shoals Rhythm Section and produced 211 charted singles, 83 top-10 records, and 14 No. 1 hits. From Reynolds Aluminum worker to acclaimed music producer, Hall's career illuminates his significant contributions to popular music. (Photograph courtesy of FAME Studios.)

Pictured in front of the original Muscle Shoals Sound Studio on Jackson Highway are, from left to right, (first row) Cher; (second row) Eddie Hinton, David Hood, Sonny Bono, Jerry Wexler, Jeannie Green, Donna Thatcher, and Tom Dowd; (third row) Jimmy Johnson, Arif Mardin, Roger Hawkins, and Barry Beckett. Cher traveled to a small town in North Alabama called Muscle Shoals to record her album *3614 Jackson Highway* in April 1969 (aptly named after the address of the studio). This photograph was to be the original album cover, but the label decided to add the address across the top of the building. The studio owners liked the look so much they went on to have a sign made to match the album cover. It still hangs there today. (Photograph courtesy of David Hood.)

Two members of the elite Muscle Shoals Rhythm Section, Barry Beckett (center) and David Hood, are seated with Cher at the piano during the *3614 Jackson Highway* sessions. (Photograph courtesy of David Hood.)

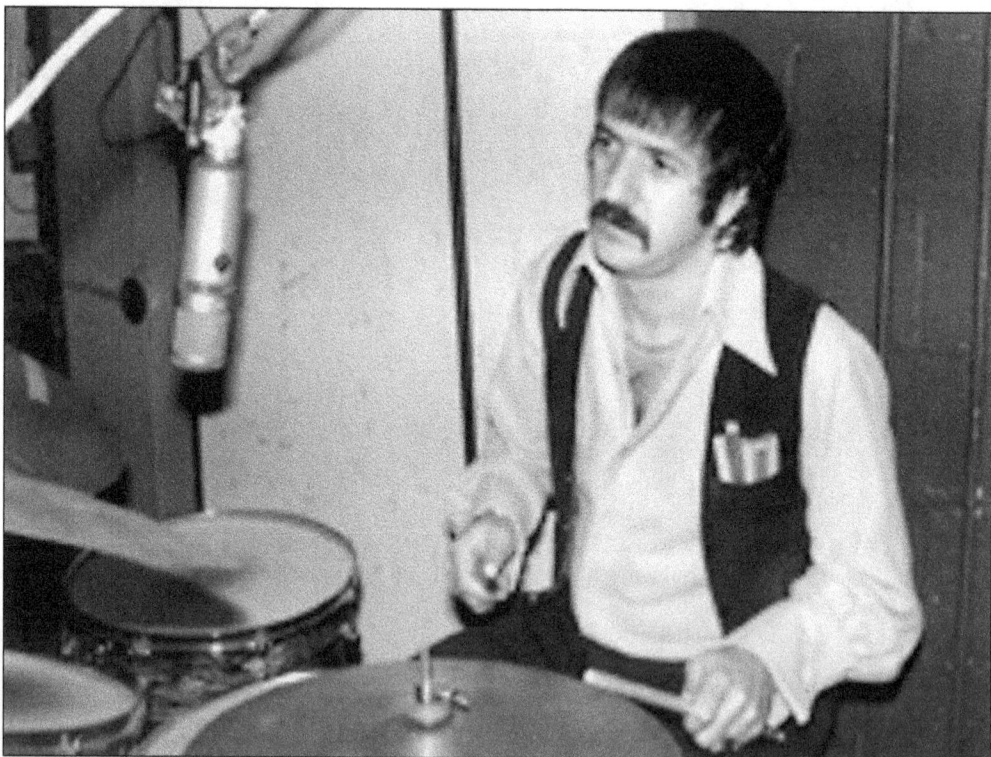

During the recording of Cher's *3614 Jackson Highway* album, her husband, Sonny Bono, was no stranger to the studio. (Photograph courtesy of David Hood.)

Initially part of FAME's in-house band, the Muscle Shoals Horns ventured out and made a name for themselves. In the 1970s, they toured extensively with Elton John and played on the "Philadelphia Freedom" recording, which also featured John Lennon. They later released three albums of their own compositions and spent some time opening for a variety of bands, one being Parliament Funkadelic. (Photograph courtesy of David Hood.)

Harvey Thompson is one of the original members of the famous Muscle Shoals Horns. Thompson has played on recordings with James Brown, Rod Stewart, Waylon Jennings, Hank Williams Jr., Isaac Hayes, Alabama, the late Roy Orbison, Dolly Parton, and many more. Currently Thompson tours with Lyle Lovett. (Photograph courtesy of David Hood.)

Atlantic Records executive Jerry Wexler (left) coined the phrase "Rhythm and Blues" in the 1940s as a young writer for Billboard Magazine. His partnership with Willie Nelson began when he signed Nelson in 1972 and chose the Muscle Shoals Sound Studio to record Nelson's *Phases and Stages* album. Wexler was initially criticized for choosing Muscle Shoals. "Everyone in Nashville thought I was out of my mind. They said Muscle Shoals was too R&B for Willie. I said Willie was too R&B for Nashville." (Photograph courtesy of Dick Cooper.)

Bob Dylan (center) recorded his 1979 release *Slow Train Coming* in Muscle Shoals. He is pictured with Atlantic Records executive Jerry Wexler (right) and Muscle Shoals Rhythm Section keyboardist Barry Beckett, who share the production credit on this album. "The best part of my career was not the gold records or the Hall of Fame or awards," Wexler said, "it was hearing the music being recorded live at that time." (Photograph courtesy of Dick Cooper.)

Pictured from left to right are (at the soundboard) Greg Hamm, Barry Beckett, and Mark Knoffler; (second row) Bob Dylan and Jerry Wexler. Jerry Wexler played a significant role in the development of the Muscle Shoals recording industry by bringing acts like Wilson Pickett and Aretha Franklin in the mid-1960s and by funding the opening of the Muscle Shoals Sound Studio in 1969. (Photograph courtesy of David Hood.)

Hailed as one of the greatest guitar players of all time, Duane Allman, cofounder of the legendary Allman Brothers, worked as a session musician in Muscle Shoals. His performance on Wilson Pickett's "Hey Jude" got the attention of Rick Hall, who alerted Atlantic Records executive Jerry Wexler. Wexler, in turn, hired Allman to play on a series of albums for renowned artists, most of which were recorded in Muscle Shoals. The list of luminaries includes Clarence Carter, Percy Sledge, Boz Scaggs, and the great Aretha Franklin. (Photograph courtesy of FAME Studios.)

Duane Allman was photographed during a recording session in the Muscle Shoals studio in the late 1960s. His astounding ability placed him on Rolling Stone's guitarist list, second only to Jimi Hendrix. (Photograph courtesy of David Hood.)

The fall of 1972 brought the popular 1960s and 1970s rock band Traffic to Muscle Shoals to record their *Shoot Out at the Fantasy Factory* album. Adding bassist David Hood and drummer Roger Hawkins, along with other members of the renowned Muscle Shoals recording studio, Steve Winwood and the band delivered their fourth consecutive studio album, which hit the American Top Ten and would go gold. Traffic was inducted into the Rock and Roll Hall of Fame in 2004. (Photograph courtesy of David Hood.)

The draw of the outstanding session players in Muscle Shoals brought Grammy-winner Art Garfunkel in 1978 to record his *Watermark* album. Keyboardist Barry Beckett coproduced it. Included on this album was Sam Cooke's classic "What a Wonderful World." (Photograph courtesy of David Hood.)

Known as half of the world-famous Simon and Garfunkel duo, Paul Simon embarked on a highly successful solo career in 1970. "Kodachrome," from his 1973 album *There Goes Rhymin' Simon*, reached No. 2 on the U.S. charts and was recorded in Muscle Shoals with the Rhythm Section. (Photograph courtesy of David Hood.)

Regarded as one of the greatest soul singers of all time, Etta James found her way to FAME Studios in 1968, where she recorded what many consider her most accomplished album, *Tell Mama*. Produced by Rick Hall and backed by the legendary session players, this album turned out songs like "The Love of My Man," "Watch Dog," and the heartbreaking "I'd Rather Go Blind." In 2001, a reissue of this album was released with the subtitle "The Complete Muscle Shoals Sessions," which included 10 previously unreleased tracks. (Photograph courtesy of FAME Studios.)

Linda Ronstadt's self-titled 1972 album propelled her career as one of the biggest rock stars of the decade. Recording at the Muscle Shoals Sound Studio, Ronstadt was backed by the exemplary session players, along with future Eagles members Glen Fry and Don Henley. (Photograph courtesy of David Hood.)

The Oak Ridge Boys, two-time Grammy winners, spent some time in the Muscle Shoals Sound Studio working with members of the Muscle Shoals Rhythm Section in the 1980s. (Photograph courtesy of David Hood.)

After exploding on the music scene in the 1950s and laying the groundwork for what would become known as rock and roll, the charismatic Little Richard took time off to attend a Bible college in Huntsville, Alabama. Following this musical hiatus, Little Richard headed to Muscle Shoals to record what has been called one of the greatest comeback rock and roll albums in history, *The Rill Thing*, released in 1970. Inducted into the Rock and Roll Hall of Fame in 1986, this musical pioneer remains a pop icon. (Photographs courtesy of FAME Studios.)

Best known for writing "Sitting on the Dock of the Bay," the influential rhythm-and-blues singer/songwriter/producer Otis Redding (left) spent time in the Muscle Shoals FAME Studios. Acting primarily as a producer, Otis is pictured during a recording session at the sound board with Rick Hall. One of Redding's only known recordings in Muscle Shoals was a demo of "You Left the Water Running," which was released many years later in a CD box set. The photograph below shows Wilson Pickett in the studio at FAME, where he recorded such classics as "Mustang Sally," "Land of 1,000 Dances," and "Hey Jude." (Photographs courtesy of FAME Studios.)

Rick Hall earned the title "Billboard's Producer of the Year" in 1971 for his work with the Osmonds. Hall produced two albums, *The Osmonds* and *Homemade*, along with consecutive hit singles "One Bad Apple" and "Yo Yo," which in total sold 11 million records in a single year. The Osmonds have proven to be one of the longest-running family dynasties in popular music. In the span of seven years (1971–1978) they accumulated 23 gold records. With careers spanning well over 30 years, the Osmonds continue to perform to this day. (Photographs courtesy of FAME Studios.)

Following the Osmonds' tremendous success, Bobbie Gentry found her way to FAME Studios in Muscle Shoals and recorded the 1970 pop-country hit "Fancy." Gentry originally burst on the international music scene in 1968 with "Ode to Billie Joe." The milk cow her grandmother traded for her first piano really paid off. (Photograph courtesy of FAME Studios.)

Atlantic Records executive and producer Jerry Wexler is pictured with Mick Jagger (left) at an industry event. Wexler had strong ties to the Muscle Shoals studio and helped to facilitate the recordings the Rolling Stones made here. Wexler was inducted into the Rock and Roll Hall of Fame in 1987. The Rolling Stones followed two years later, receiving the title of "The World's Greatest Rock and Roll Band." (Photograph courtesy of David Hood.)

December 1969 brought the Rolling Stones to the Muscle Shoals Sound Studio to begin recording their *Sticky Fingers* album. "We wrote the chorus of ['Wild Horses'] in the john of the Muscle Shoals recording studio," said Keith Richards in a 1971 interview. "You Gotta Move" and chart topper "Brown Sugar" were also recorded during the Muscle Shoals sessions. (Photograph courtesy of David Hood.)

Rolling Stones bassist Bill Wyman pauses during the Muscle Shoals December sessions. (Photograph courtesy of David Hood.)

Footage from the Muscle Shoals jaunt can be seen in the Rolling Stones' infamous documentary of 1970's *Gimme Shelter*, which resulted in the death of four fans at the Altamont Speedway in Northern California. David Hood recalls trying to keep the Stones' visit to Muscle Shoals quiet. "We were naïve enough not to try and capitalize it at the time." The recording sessions took place during the Stones' 1969 American tour. "The Muscle Shoals Studio was very special, though—a great studio to work in, a very hip studio, where the drums were on a riser high up in the air, plus you wanted to be there because of all the guys who had worked in the same studio," said Stones drummer Charlie Watts in 2003. Mick Jagger is pictured at the soundboard and playing the maracas on the "Brown Sugar" track. (Photographs courtesy of David Hood.)

Aretha Franklin was encouraged by Jerry Wexler to come to Muscle Shoals to record her 1967 single "I Never Loved A Man (The Way I Loved You)." After a dispute with Rick Hall, she ended her sessions with FAME and went on to record with the Muscle Shoals Rhythm Section. The gritty soulful R&B sound the Rhythm Section produced melded perfectly with Aretha's passion and intensity. Brilliantly matched, this combination turned out Aretha's most well-known smash, "Respect," among numerous others. All together, the Rhythm Section backed Aretha on at least 15 titles. "It seemed we could do nothing but make good records," says Atlantic Records executive Jerry Wexler. "We had this little hideaway, this little retreat with these terrific musicians, these incredible white boys who played the blues so authentically that it caused a lot of head scratching." (Photograph courtesy of David Hood.)

The Staple Singers recorded some of their classic songs like "If You're Ready," "Come Go With Me," and "Respect Yourself" in Muscle Shoals. As the story goes, Paul Simon journeyed to the Shoals in 1973 to work with the black musicians that backed the Staple Singers on their No. 1 hit "I'll Take You There." Unbeknownst to him, the players were four white guys. This is a perfect example of the Rhythm Section's ability to turn out this funky Southern soul-infused sound that would continually draw world-famous musicians, singers, and industry executives to the unlikely town of Muscle Shoals. Seen at right are Pops and Mavis Staples. Below, Rhythm Section bassist David Hood is pictured with Mavis Staples, who is wearing a Muscle Shoals Sound T-shirt. (Photographs courtesy of David Hood.)

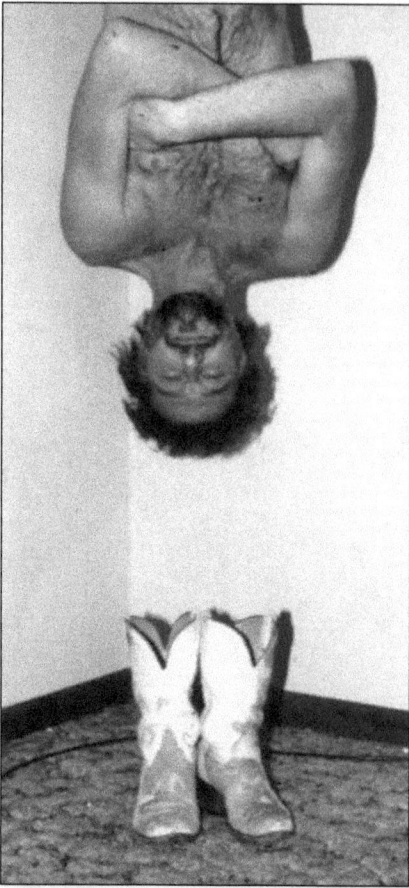

Jerry Jeff Walker is a singer/songwriter best known as the man who penned and recorded "Mr. Bojangles" in 1968. Session player Barry Beckett produced Jerry Jeff Walker. Bob Dylan and Sammy Davis Jr., among many others, have covered and recorded "Mr. Bojangles." (Photograph courtesy of Dick Cooper.)

Pictured is Lynyrd Skynyrd with a group of locals who turned up in response to an advertisement in the local paper for back-up singers. Everyone who showed up got to sing back-up on a "Free Bird" recording with the band. Each person was given a certificate that stated they were an official Lynyrd Skynyrd band member for a day. It was signed by all of the actual band members. (Photograph Courtesy of Dick Cooper.)

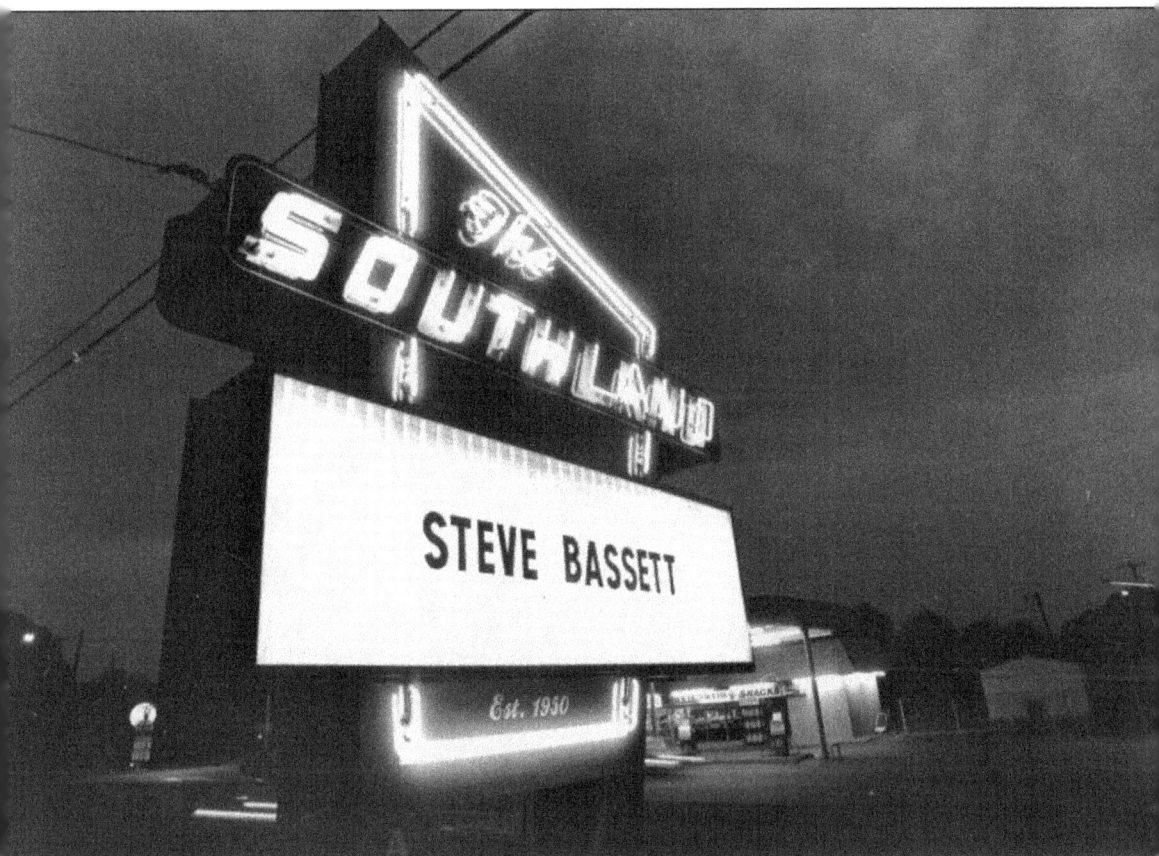

The Southland is a local meat-and-three restaurant that was a popular dining spot for musicians during long recording sessions. As the story goes, the Rolling Stones were there having dinner clad in outlandish snakeskin and boas when a waitress asked if they were in a band. Bassist Bill Wyman replied matter-of-factly, "Yes. We're Martha and the Vandellas." The anonymity with which massive music stars could move in and out of town was quite possibly a small part of the Muscle Shoals attraction. "[Muscle Shoals] is just a lot more laid back than any other music center in the country," says FAME Studios president Rodney Hall. Something about this town was appealing, since the stars just kept coming. (Photograph courtesy of David Hood.)

Visitors have been known to travel from all over the world to have their picture made in front of this studio. Some are said to have come from as far as England to see the renowned studio where musical history was created. The building itself is said to be an old casket warehouse that eventually became referred to as the "burlap palace." Pictured is the Muscle Shoals Rhythm Section with all the Muscle Shoals Sound songwriters. (Photograph courtesy of David Hood.)

Continuing the musical legacy of his father (Rhythm Section bassist David Hood), Patterson Hood and his band, the Drive-By Truckers, are turning the rock industry's eye back towards Muscle Shoals. Four of the five band members are Shoals-area natives. The Southern rockers have been together for at least a decade playing, touring, and recording across the nation. The Drive-By Truckers received their first national attention for their double-CD release *Southern Rock Opera* in 2001. *Rolling Stone* gave the album a four-star review. The Drive-By Truckers are comprised of Patterson Hood, Jason Isbell, Mike Cooley, Shonna Tucker, and Brad Morgan. (Photograph courtesy of Adam Smith.)

The Muscle Shoals Sound Studio closed in 2005, but Patterson Hood maintains the unique chemistry created here. "I don't want the closing of Muscle Shoals Sound to make anyone think that music is no longer happening here," says Hood. "It has been happening since before I started, and it is still going on today. It was always the people." Patterson Hood is pictured at a show in Atlanta, Georgia, in 2006. (Photograph courtesy of Adam Smith.)

Pictured with Barry Beckett (top) and Bonnie Bramlett is Delbert McClinton (front). McClinton was signed to a branch of Capitol Records, MSS-Capitol, which was developed when the Rhythm Section opened its new studio in 1978. He is known as a Texas-born writer, vocalist, and harmonica player, but he is probably best recognized as always in the pocket (always brings exactly the right thing to the moment in the music) and often ahead of his time. (Photograph courtesy of Dick Cooper.)

Blues Hall of Fame member Little Milton (second from left) is pictured with Gov't Mule. Fusing country with gospel and blues, Little Milton is a prolific talent. Warren Haynes, guitarist and vocalist of Gov't Mule (right), can hold his own in good company. Gov't Mule recorded their soulful, gritty sounds at Muscle Shoals Studios as part of their fifth album, *Life Before Insanity.* (Photograph courtesy of Dick Cooper.)

Charles Rose was one of the acclaimed Muscle Shoals Horns. Joining in the 1970s on trombone, he played with the Alabama Music Hall of Fame group into the 1980s. In addition, he is a key member of the community when it comes to environmental preservation. He has served as the president of the Shoals Environmental Alliance, which established an interpretive native-plant garden at TVA's Muscle Shoals/Wilson Dam Reservation in Alabama. (Photograph courtesy of Dick Cooper.)

Since 1982, the W. C. Handy Festival has been presented each summer by the Music Preservation Society and the Muscle Shoals Music Association (MSMA). The Music Preservation Society is non-profit and serves to "preserve, present and promote the musical heritage of Northwest Alabama." Education is a strong mission for the society as well. The MSMA has been growing strong since its establishment in 1975 as an outgrowth of the prolific music scene in the Shoals. (Photograph courtesy of Library of Congress.)

Visit us at
arcadiapublishing.com